• • THE LIBRARY OF FAMOUS WOMEN • •

BETTE DAVIS

Film Star

by
Gene Brown

A BLACKBIRCH PRESS BOOK

WOODBRIDGE, CONNECTICUT

Published by Blackbirch Press, Inc.
One Bradley Road, Suite 205
Woodbridge, CT 06525

©1990 Blackbirch Press, Inc.
First Edition

Manufactured in the United States of America

10 9 8 7 6 5 4 3 2 1

Library of Congress Cataloging-in-Publication Data

Brown, Gene.
  Bette Davis: film star / Gene Brown.
  (The Library of famous women)
  Includes bibliographical references and index.
  Summary: A biography of the renowned movie actress whose film career spanned more than fifty years.
  ISBN 1-56711-028-2
  1. Davis, Bette, 1908–1989—Juvenile literature. 2. Motion picture actors and actresses—United States—Biography—Juvenile literature. [1. Davis, Bette, 1908–1989. 2. Actors and actresses.] I. Title. II. Series.
PN2287.D32B76 1990
791.43'028'092—dc20
[92]
[B]
90-40556
CIP
AC

Contents

Chapter 1

Becoming an Actress

Bette Davis acted in movies for more than fifty years. In the mid-1940s she was America's most famous female movie star. She was also one of its most unusual ones.

Davis started acting in movies in the early 1930s. Then, even more than now, people wanted movie stars to be beautiful. Talent wasn't as important as beauty. Although many people found Bette Davis attractive, almost no one said that she was beautiful. Her first Hollywood boss called her "that skinny thing with the pop eyes."

Strong Roles for a Strong Woman

Bette's talent and strong personality rather than how she looked brought her success. "I brought more people into the theaters than all the sexpots put together," she once said. She was probably right. She reached the top because she dared to take

(At left)
Bette Davis was the first woman who played roles that portrayed women realistically.

chances. Few famous actresses in her day wanted to play characters who were bad. Bette was different. She was the first major star willing to play women who were selfish, nasty, even evil.

Sometimes she played women who were soft and weak. More often her characters were tough and hard. Davis took parts like this in many of her more than eighty films. Now we take it for granted that actresses will be willing to play tough women. When Bette was young, however, many actresses thought that such roles would ruin their careers. They were afraid that the public wouldn't like the women they played—and because of that would not like *them.*

All of Bette Davis's directors were men. They were used to having their own way, especially with women. Bette was different. If she disagreed with a director about how to play a scene, she fought to do it her way. When Bette felt that the people at the movie studio where she worked didn't treat her fairly she stood up to them. In fact, she would walk out. She was the first major female star to do so. She fought long and hard for what she wanted. Because of this many people said that she was difficult to work with. She believed she was just being true to herself.

Off the screen, Bette Davis also went her own way. In those days women weren't supposed to curse, but she did. She also smoked when it was still a little unusual for so-called nice girls to do that. Worse still, in many people's minds, she believed her career was just as important as any man's.

Being a rebel had its price. Few women then dared to live as they wished. Most women thought of a happy marriage as their main goal in life. Husbands expected their wives to stay at home, take care of the children and the house, and devote themselves to supporting their husband's career. Men assumed that they would make all the important decisions in the family. Bette was too independent to fully accept this way of living, and this was partly the reason for her four unhappy marriages.

In Her Mother's Footsteps

Bette was a lot like her mother, Ruthie Davis, who was strong minded and independent. Ruthie had acted in school plays and had hoped to become an actress, a career that *her* mother, Bette's grandmother, wouldn't permit. She believed that the stage was not a proper place for a decent girl. So she pushed Ruthie into a marriage with a lawyer, Harlow Davis.

Bette *(left)* and her sister, Bobby, at the beach.

Their first child was Bette. She was born Ruth Elizabeth Davis in 1908 in Lowell, Massachusetts. Her father had not wanted to have children right away. He thought it might interfere with his career. So he was not happy when his wife became pregnant with Bette soon after their marriage. He wanted to give the baby up for adoption. Abortion was then both illegal and out of the question for someone from a respectable background.

Mr. Davis did not show much affection to Bette and her sister, Bobby. Nor was he very close to his wife as time went on. They separated when Bette was seven. Bette later said that the divorce left her angry at her father and also made her feel much closer to her mother.

Ruthie now had to work at many jobs to support her two daughters and herself. That meant a lot of moving around. Besides changing her address often, the young Ruth Elizabeth Davis also changed her name. At the suggestion of one of her mother's friends, she started using the name "Bette."

Bette got her first chance to act in boarding school. It almost caused a real-life tragedy. She was playing Santa Claus and was accidentally burned on the face by some Christmas candles. The burns healed, but for the rest of her life her skin would be very sensitive to the sun and to makeup. This would sometimes cause problems when she had to make a movie outdoors. She also had to be very careful when she was made up for a film.

As Bette got older, she became more serious about acting. All through high school she appeared in school plays. If Bette wanted to act, that was all right with her mother. Ruthie remembered what it felt like when her mother dashed her own hopes of being an actress. Seeing Bette on the stage also allowed Ruthie to feel as if she herself were up there. She could live the life of an actress through her daughter.

The best school for acting was in New York. Eva La Gallienne, a famous actress, ran it. To get in, students had to try out. So Ruthie took Bette to the school for an acting test. It didn't work out. Bette was nervous, and she and Eva La Gallienne did not hit it off.

The first defeat did not stop Bette and her mother. Bette finally got into the John Murray Anderson acting school in New York. The school even gave her a scholarship. There she studied dance as well as acting.

From Stage to Hollywood

Bette's professional acting career began in Rochester, New York, in 1928. Just out of acting school, she got a part in a play called *Broadway.* Its director, George Cukor, later became a famous movie director.

Cukor liked Bette's work. He said she acted with a kind of "white heat." She was already showing some of the energy that people would see in her on the movie screen. But Cukor also felt that Bette was too sassy. She was too quick to talk back. They didn't get along. So Bette did not stay in Rochester for long.

Bette next acted in a play at the famous Provincetown Playhouse in New York City's Greenwich Village. She got good reviews, which led to a part in a hit Broadway play called *Broken Dishes.* Again the critics liked her.

She was becoming well known. In Hollywood, the MGM movie studio heard about her. They asked her to take a screen test— a tryout for a movie contract. She flunked the test.

Bette and her mother, Ruthie, at the premiere of *All This and Heaven Too* (1940).

Bette's mother kept urging her daughter to keep at it. All through Bette's early career, Ruthie was her daughter's biggest fan. "I owe everything to her," Bette later said of her mother.

Ruthie's support of Bette's career paid off in 1930. Bette was asked to take another screen test. This time the call came from Universal Studios. They liked what they saw. So mother and daughter got on a train to Los Angeles. They were on their way to Hollywood. The trip would change Bette Davis's life. It would also change movie history.

Chapter 2

On the Edge of Stardom

A man waited at the Los Angeles train station to hand Bette a bunch of flowers. This was Universal's way of welcoming a new actress to Hollywood. Finally, not seeing the person he was looking for, he returned to the studio still holding the flowers. Meanwhile, Bette and her mother checked into a hotel. They called Universal to find out why no one had met them at the train. They were told that the man with the flowers had seen no one get off the train who *looked* like a movie star.

The studio's makeup man made her feel even worse. He said that Bette's mouth was "too small" and her neck "too long." "They didn't know what to do with me," she said later on. "I was an odd-looking person."

Bette's first job was to lie on a couch while fifteen men, one after another, pretended to romance her. They were taking a screen test for a movie part, and she was simply there to help them out. Finally, the studio put Bette in a movie. *Bad Sister*, her first film, was nothing to brag about. Carl Laemmle, Jr., who ran Universal, said that the movie was "very bad." Bette knew that as soon as she saw it. In fact, she cried at the preview. Years later, though, she said that it was so bad it was funny. "If you ever saw it," she told an interviewer, "you would roll on the floor laughing."

Bette Enters the Studio System

In the two years she spent working for Universal, Bette Davis only made a few minor, forgettable movies. One lucky thing, though, did happen to her there. A cameraman noticed that she had very pretty eyes. He mentioned this to an actor working in another studio. The actor, George Arliss, needed a leading lady for his next film. He decided that Bette was just the person he was looking for.

Arliss had already had a long acting career, and he was very respected. He got in touch with Bette just in time. Universal had already told her that they would not use her in any more of their movies, and

Bette Davis and Dick Powell during a radio broadcast of "Your Hollywood Parade."

she was about to leave Hollywood. Arliss got his studio, Warner Brothers, to hire Bette for his film.

This movie, *The Man Who Played God,* came out in 1932. Arliss took an interest in Bette's success. He made sure that the camera caught her from the best angles, and he helped her with her acting. A *New York Times* critic said that Bette talked too fast in the film, but most people liked it and her performance in it. Warner Brothers liked her enough to offer her a long-term contract. She was to stay with them for the next eighteen years. It was the studio at which she would do most of her famous movies.

Most stars were under long-term contracts to movie studios in the 1930s. Contracts guaranteed actors and actresses regular salaries. In return, the studio was able to choose which films their stars would make and how many they would do each year. Sometimes the studio made actors and actresses work in as many as eight to ten films in a year. There were even times when they had to work on more than one film at a time.

The studios created an image for each of their stars—a certain look or personality trait—that audiences would like and remember. Studio publicity departments gave stories about their stars to the movie fan magazines. These stories made their subjects seem very romantic, interesting, and colorful off the screen as well as on. A studio might even change a person's name or appearance if they thought that it would be more appealing. Warner Brothers decided to bleach Bette Davis's already blond hair. They also altered her makeup to better reflect her eyes, her best feature.

The studio had complete control over a person's working and personal life. Studios could lend out an actress or actor to another studio for one or more films. For example, another movie studio, like MGM, might want to use Bette Davis in a film. If that was all right with Warner Brothers, her studio, MGM could make a deal for her services. Bette had no say in the matter, and Warner Brothers kept all the profits from the work she did. All this was known as the "studio system."

A Star Is Born

Bette's first few films at Warners after *The Man Who Played God* were nothing special, although one featured her as an independent woman, the kind of role she liked. This film was *Cabin in the Cotton*,

Bette Davis and Mickey Rooney (left) being crowned King and Queen of Hollywood by famous journalist and radio talk-show host, Ed Sullivan.

Bette Davis with Gene Raymond, her co-star, in a scene from *Ex-Lady* (1933).

made in 1932. The character she plays almost destroys the hero. When he gets romantic, Bette puts him off with a line that would become famous. She tells him, "Ah'd love to kiss ya, but ah jes' washed mah hair."

In the movie *Ex-Lady,* made in 1933, Bette earned star billing. For the first time her name appeared over the title of a film in newspaper ads and outside movie theaters. *Ex-Lady* was also the first of many films that showed the problems women faced. Bette plays an artist in *Ex-Lady* who wants to live with her boyfriend without getting married. She just doesn't believe in marriage, but he finally pushes her into it. The couple is soon in trouble when the husband can't stand the idea that his wife still wants a career. She's very unhappy, and she leaves him.

If this movie were made today, the woman Bette plays might have gone on to lead a happy and creative life. She would have been free to follow her own feelings about how she wanted to live. That, however, wasn't the message movies sent in those days. Instead, the woman is raped by the first man she dates after leaving her husband. Later, speaking to her husband, she says that she's disgusted with how men treat single women. He says "that's how it will always be when a wife leaves her husband—for any reason." Feeling defeated, she returns to him and the unhappy marriage.

"Every actor who becomes a star is usually remembered for one or two roles," Bette once said. The role that would make Bette a star was in the film *Of Human Bondage.* It was made by another studio, RKO. The director of the film at RKO had seen some of Bette's movies and wanted her for this one.

There was a lot of pain and suffering in this movie. It was about a medical student, Philip, who falls in love with a waitress, Mildred, who is then very mean to him. Mildred makes fun of Philip because he has a twisted foot. She knows that he has fallen in love with her, but she tells him that she is going to marry another man. This other man gets her pregnant and then leaves her. She goes back to Philip, who still loves her and is willing to take care of her. Meanwhile, another woman, who is decent and who truly loves Philip, gives up on him because he can't seem to get Mildred out of his life.

Mildred repays Philip's kindness by going out and getting pregnant by another medical student. Again she's abandoned. This time Philip says that he's had it with her. Mildred then wrecks his apartment. Philip finally finds happiness with another

him back to earth aga[...]

LESLIE
HOWARD
"OF HUMAN
BONDAGE

BETTE DAVIS
FRANCES DEE
KAY JOHNSON
REGINALD DENNY

WITH
DIRECTED BY JOHN CROMWELL
PANDRO S. BERMAN
PRODUCTION

woman. The story ends when Philip hears that Mildred is dying.

At first, Warner Brothers said "no" to Bette making this film. They thought that it would not be good for her career—and their investment in her. They didn't want her playing too many bad women. But she

A poster from *Of Human Bondage* (1934). Bette plays an angry working-class girl who rejects a well-to-do medical student.

Bette models a dress she wore in the film *Satan Met a Lady* (1936).

knew that "villains always have the best written parts." She wanted the role. She kept asking, and they finally gave in. Thinking she was making a big mistake, her boss told her, "Go hang yourself."

Bette decided that there was only one way to play Mildred: "no glamour." She refused even to go near a beauty parlor while making the film. Very few actresses would have dared to do that. "I was one of the first who wanted to look like a real person," she later said.

As for what kind of person she was playing, Bette had no doubts: "Mildred *had* to be a bitch." The critics had no doubts about what kind of acting Bette did in the movie. *Life* magazine later called it "Probably the best performance ever recorded on the screen by a U.S. actress."

Fame in the Midst of Unhappiness

Bette's personal life at this time, although not quite as rough as the one she acted on the screen, was far from ideal. She once called herself a "romantic fool."

In 1932 Bette married Ham Nelson, a musician she had known since she was a teenager. Just when she was trying to convince Warner Brothers to let her do *Of Human Bondage*, Bette became pregnant.

Both her husband and her mother thought it was the wrong time for her to have a child. She had an abortion, the first of several. "I did as I was told," she later said.

Although Bette often did what she was told, she seemed to be of two minds about men. She wanted the man in her life to do the kinds of things that men were supposed to do—take care of her, for example. She wanted a man she could look up to, someone who would earn more money than she did. On the other hand, she wanted total control of her life—and the people in it.

Everybody, including herself, expected her to be a normal wife. In the 1930s, such a woman stayed home and took care of the house, her husband, and her children. A wife took a back seat to her husband. But Bette, who was talented and ambitious, also wanted to make her own mark on the world. She didn't want to be number two in her own home. She could never bring these conflicting feelings together.

Ham did not earn much. He made about one-tenth of what Bette did. He also had a weak personality. It did not help when people called him "Mr. Davis," as if Bette were the boss. Bette had little respect for him. Sometimes she treated him a little bit like Mildred treated Philip in *Of Human Bondage.* Her marriage with Ham went downhill quickly.

Fortunately, Bette was able to keep her mind on her work even when she had problems at home. It was during these troubled years that she gave a good performance in the film *Bordertown.* This movie was made before *Of Human Bondage,* but came out after it, in 1935. While making *Bordertown* Bette had one of her first fights with a director.

There is a scene at the end of the film in which the woman she plays is in court. She's nervous and upset. While she's on the witness stand, she goes to pieces. The director wanted Bette to ham it up. But she thought she should act more like a real person would. She talked the studio into letting her do it her way. Then they showed it to an audience at a preview. The people liked the scene, and it stayed the way Bette played it.

In 1935 Bette made another movie, called *Front Page Woman.* A male reporter, played by George Brent, thinks that Bette, who plays a woman reporter, would be better off as a housewife. Her editor says that women writers should be writing the little sayings on birthday cards instead of working on a newspaper. Bette's character wins out and proves both of them wrong. She shows that a woman can be just as good a reporter as a man.

Another film she made that year, *Dangerous,* was a soap opera about a star, down on her luck, who makes a comeback. The critics didn't think much of the picture, but Bette got rave reviews for her acting. One critic felt that her performance was so powerful that it was almost superhuman. "Bette Davis would probably have been burned as a witch if she had lived two or three hundred years ago," he wrote.

Oscar winners Bette Davis and Victor McLaglen, 1936.

Then a strange thing happened. Many people felt that Bette deserved an Oscar for best actress for the movie *Of Human Bondage.* She was heartbroken when she didn't get the award. She thought she lost out because Warner Brothers had not made the film and therefore the studio didn't fight for her.

A year later, Hollywood made it up to her. She won the best actress award for *Dangerous.* It was the first of two such awards she would win.

In *The Petrified Forest,* which Bette made in 1936, Humphrey Bogart played a vicious killer. It was the role that made him famous. Bette also did a good job, but making the film was hard on her. They did a lot of filming in the desert. The sun was rough on her sensitive skin and the dust made her sick. By the time they finished the film she was tired. "I need a rest," she told the company, "my nerves are frayed."

Warner Brothers ignored her request, and they sent her the script for another film that they wanted her to make. The studio pressed her to do it. The movie did not look promising, but she didn't have much choice.

At the time, Bette had a lot on her mind. Besides trouble with her marriage, she also had some money problems. She was making about $1,000 a week, a lot of money for that time, but she also owed a lot. Her sister, Bobby, was mentally ill. Bobby had to be hospitalized often, and Bette paid the bills. Bette was also supporting her mother, Ruthie, who was developing expensive taste in clothes, cars, and furniture.

Bette made the film her studio offered her: *Satan Met a Lady.* As she had predicted, it wasn't very good. Little of what Warners was now asking Bette to do was of high quality. She felt she was going nowhere, but her contract kept her from striking out on her own. It said that she couldn't work for anyone else unless the studio gave its permission. When it came down to it, she had to do what Warner Brothers told her to do.

Winning the Oscar, however, made her bold. When the next movie they asked her to do cast her as a lumberjack, she refused to take the part. She defied the studio. She told her bosses that she wanted "to be known as a great actress. I *might* be one. Who can tell?" The public would never know, unless she could play better roles. All she got from Warner Brothers was "bad scripts, bad directors." She said that her career was going "downhill," and she felt "desperate."

The Showdown

Bette demanded to have more control over which movies she made. She insisted on longer vacations and more money— $3,000 a week. Warner Brothers said that they would meet her halfway. They offered her $2,000 a week. They also made a vague promise to improve her working conditions.

The studio also tried to tempt Bette with an offer she couldn't turn down. They had just bought the rights to a novel that they thought would make a great movie. They offered her the lead role. "You were born to play the heroine," Jack Warner, who ran the studio, told her. In no mood to give in, Bette replied, "Sure, I'll bet it's a pip." She didn't take them seriously. It was probably the biggest mistake of her career. The movie they wanted her to do was *Gone With the Wind,* one of the greatest films Hollywood ever turned out.

Warner Brothers and their rising star were now stuck. The studio felt that they couldn't give in to Bette's demands. They felt that if they gave in, every star would start demanding whatever they wanted. The studio system would fall apart. Jack Warner gave Bette a warning. He told her that breaking her contract would get her in trouble. "Change your mind before it's too late!" he said.

Bette felt just as strongly that if she did what they asked, she would never be a great actress. Finally, she made her move. She signed an agreement to make two movies for another company. Then she sailed for England, where the films were to be made.

The studio suspended her and cut off her salary. They also took her to court. Since Bette was working in England, the trial was in an English court. Warner Brothers said

Bette had broken her contract. It asked the judge to order her not to make movies for anyone else.

The studio's lawyer said that what Bette was doing was "the action of a very naughty young lady." Bette answered that the studio treated her like a "slave." The studio's lawyer did call her Warner Brothers's "personal servant."

Bette's lawyer pointed out just how much of a slave she was. Under her contract, the studio could make her appear in a radio commercial or in a newspaper ad. She couldn't refuse. They could tell her to appear at a political convention. It didn't matter if it was for a political party she didn't like. They could even prevent her from getting a divorce for a certain number of years.

To nobody's surprise, Warner Brothers won the case. They had it all in writing; the law was on their side. Bette had signed a contract. It was legal, and that was all there was to it.

What now? George Arliss, the actor who had helped Bette to make it in the movies, gave her some advice. "Take your medicine," he told her. She had lost. Now she had to go back to work for Warner Brothers.

Chapter 3

Back in Business

In a way, walking out helped Bette make her point with Warner Brothers. The reviews of *Satan Met a Lady* were bad. The studio realized that Bette had been right. They were not doing well by their most promising actress. So they started treating her better, giving her more respect. They now made an effort to get her better stories for the movies she played in. This helped both Bette and the studio.

"Bad" Women Make for Good Roles

Her next film, *Marked Woman*, was a good one. It was about a gangster who forced young women to work for him as prostitutes. Warner Brothers had become known as the studio that dealt with real social problems in its films. However, movies during this time could not directly portray subjects like prostitution. So

Marked Woman only hints that the women were prostitutes.

When Bette stands up to the gangster because he has caused the death of her sister, she is beaten. Instead of wearing the kind of bandages that Hollywood usually used, she went to her own doctor and asked him to bandage her as if she had really been beaten. She wanted to look as true-to-life as possible.

In the movie her courage and example helps the other women to fight back. They go to the district attorney, played by Humphrey Bogart. He puts an end to the gangster's business.

The movie ends with the women leaving court and walking off together into the night. What does the future hold for them? Can they avoid having someone else take advantage of them? We don't know.

While Bette was getting a reputation for arguing with directors, she was also becoming known for helping her co-stars. In *Marked Woman,* Jane Bryan, a young actress playing Bette's sister, was nervous about her role. Bette looked after her and tried to make things as easy as possible for her. Bryan later called her "the most unselfish star I could imagine."

Bette receiving the Volpi Cup, an award given by the Italian government, for her outstanding dramatic performances in *Marked Woman* (1937) and *Kid Galahad* (1937).

By 1938, Bette Davis was one of Hollywood's top actresses. That year she made *Jezebel.* The movie is still popular, and it is often shown on TV. Its director, William Wyler, was one of Hollywood's best. Bette was not used to doing any scene in a movie more than once or twice, but Wyler insisted on doing everything as many times as it took to get it right—take after take until it was perfect. He was as much a perfectionist as Bette. The result was her second Oscar for best actress.

Jezebel takes place around the time of the Civil War. Bette plays a southern woman who is full of spirit and likes to do things her own way. She does daring things, like wearing a red dress to the ball when all unmarried girls are supposed to wear white. Bette's character also likes to flirt and get her boyfriend, played by Henry Fonda, jealous. That leads to tragedy. Fonda challenges another man, who is interested in her, to a duel and kills him. The movie ends with Fonda deathly ill. He has since married someone else, but Bette risks catching his disease to care for him when his wife can't.

More than once Bette played women who got men killed or injured. In *Dangerous*, the other film for which she won an Oscar, the character she plays is bitter because her husband won't give her a divorce. She purposely crashes their car into a tree, leaving her husband disabled. In *The Little Foxes,* made in 1941, her character watches her husband die of a heart attack. She doesn't call for help because she wants control of the family business. One fan wrote to Bette about these parts: "Why can't you be nice for a change?"

These roles Bette Davis played showed the dark side of how people then viewed women. On the one hand, women were sweet and soft, like angels. But when they tried to be too independent or wanted things that they shouldn't, they became dangerous. One critic wrote that these women, as Bette played them, were "self-centered vultures." Still, moviegoers were fascinated by such women.

Bette also found the roles interesting. She probably spoke for many women who went to see her films when she said that these characters could act in ways that weren't thought proper for women at the time. She looked forward to playing women like the one in *The Little Foxes*. It was because "they have the courage to do the brutal things I've always wanted to do but couldn't," Bette said. She didn't mean getting men killed. She was talking about women who could stand up to men—and make their own way in the world, no matter what. Women who didn't worry about being "ladies."

Lost Opportunities

About this time, Bette was offered a second chance to play the one character who most stood for this type of woman: Scarlett O'Hara in *Gone With the Wind.* Producer David O. Selznick now had the rights to make the movie. He wanted to borrow Bette from Warner Brothers for the part. Errol Flynn would play Rhett Butler, the male starring role. Flynn was famous for playing macho heroes. He was handsome and always the "ladies' man." Bette, however, didn't think much of him—personally or as an actor. She didn't consider him right for this important part. So she turned down the chance to play Scarlett.

Eventually, Clark Gable, not Errol Flynn, got the role of Rhett Butler. The movie became an all-time classic. Looking back on her decision, Bette had nothing but regrets. "I had walked out on one of the greatest woman's roles of all time!" she sadly remembered.

In her personal life, Bette also made a big decision. She was going to divorce Ham.

During the worst of Bette's troubles with her studio, Ham had not been by her side. He went to England with her, but left just before the trial because he wanted to get back to work. She was deeply hurt.

Her relationship with director William Wyler could have been another reason she wanted a divorce. She and Wyler fell in love during the filming of *Jezebel*. He wanted her to leave Ham to marry him. But when she put him off, Wyler married someone else. In one of the books she later wrote about her life, *The Lonely Life*, Bette told of a mystery man who was the great love of her life. Wyler may well have been that man.

In general, this was a time of great stress for Bette. *Jezebel* was behind schedule, and she had to work on Christmas Eve. On top of that, Bette's father died and she couldn't even make time to go to his funeral. Her skin broke out in a rash, and she came down with the flu.

On top of all this, Ham found out about his wife's relationships with other men. His jealousy, coupled with Bette's unhappiness, finally brought an end to their marriage.

Chapter 4

On Top

From 1938 to 1943, Bette Davis was among Hollywood's brightest stars. In 1941, people bought more tickets for her movies than for those of any other actress. Her pictures made so much money in these years that they helped to pay for the expansion of the Warner Brothers studios. By the early 1940s she was making over $4,000 a week. Although she finally became the highest paid female star, some male stars still made three times as much as she did.

When She Talked, They Listened

She still fought with Warner Brothers, but her bosses now paid more attention to her. "Who wants to see a film about a girl who wears a red dress to a ball?" one of them asked when she wanted to make *Jezebel.* "About 10 million women," said

(At left)
In *The Little Foxes* (1941), Bette plays a former southern belle who is emotionally twisted by her greed for money.

Bette Davis for her performance in *Jezebel* **(1938) and Spencer Tracy (left) for his performance in** *Boys' Town* **(1938) were awarded the Film Academy's Golden Statuettes.**

Bette. They took her word for it and agreed to make the movie.

Bette would be nominated for an Oscar in each year from 1938 through 1942. The Academy of Motion Picture Arts and Sciences, made up of people who worked in the movies, gave this award. In 1941 they made Bette their first woman president.

Bette's lack of flashy beauty was no longer a problem. In many pictures the women she played looked attractive because, like her, they believed in themselves. They had self-respect and took themselves seriously. They had a certain power, energy, and forcefulness.

The way Bette used her body when she acted made her stand out from other movie actresses. She had quick, nervous movements. Her hands and arms, especially her elbows, moved around a lot. When she walked, she swung her hips. Her voice was a little hoarse, and she spoke almost with a clipped British accent. People loved to imitate her because she had a strong style.

As a great Hollywood star, Bette had become one of the most famous women in America. The movie fan magazines often wrote about her. They even wrote about and published pictures of her dog, a Scottie named "Tibby."

By the time she starred in *Jezebel,* Bette had made almost forty movies. But that one really put her over the top. Now people went to see her movies simply because Bette Davis was in them. In the next few years, in films like *Dark Victory, The Letter, The Little Foxes,* and *Now, Voyager,* she became the actress that women especially liked. Sometimes she played a woman who lost someone she loved or who refused to play by men's rules.

Bette's female fans seemed to identify with her roles. She acted out some of their own feelings about being in love, getting married, or having a career. In Bette's efforts on the screen to be more than just the woman behind the man in her life, many real women saw themselves. When some male critics tried to put down her films as mere "women's pictures," Bette struck back. She said "the average male has little understanding of women—on or off the screen."

This period was more than twenty years before women's liberation. So Bette's characters, after showing some independence, often gave in and acted like "ladies."

A huge marquee in Paris draws people to *Dark Victory* (1939), a film in which Bette plays the role of a dying woman.

If they didn't, they did not live happily ever after.

Bette herself, as we have seen, had mixed feelings about how independent a woman should be. She also had to be careful not to say anything that was too far from what people then believed. If she was too daring, her popularity might drop. In the late 1930s she told one fan magazine that "Women never have, never will, never can

be, independent of the men they love—
and be happy! All women know this."
How could women be happy? she was
asked. *"Men should boss women more!"* she
answered.

In her next important movie after *Jezebel,*
Bette left many people in the theaters
crying at the end. *Dark Victory* tells of a
woman who develops brain cancer and
learns that she will die from it. Her doctor,
played by George Brent, falls in love with
her and they marry. But the audience
knows that the couple can have only a brief
time together.

Bette finds out that just before her death
she will go blind. While working in her
garden, she thinks the sun has gone behind the clouds. When she realizes that
it's her sight and not the sun that's dim-
ming, she goes up to her room to be alone.
As the movie ends the picture dims, like
Bette's sight. When the image disappears,
the movie and her life are over.

No Time for Playing It Safe

Although she was now a great star and
could have played it safe, Bette kept taking
chances. She still did things most other
actresses would not have done. In two
movies in 1939, for example, she played

A love scene from *The Private Lives of Elizabeth and Essex.* **Bette stars as Queen Elizabeth I with Errol Flynn as her lover, the Earl of Essex.**

much older women. In *The Old Maid,* Bette, age thirty-one, played a woman of sixty. Unmarried when she gave birth, the character lets her daughter grow up thinking that an aunt is her mother. To keep her child respectable, she quietly suffers the pain of seeing her daughter's love go to another woman. The possibility of raising her daughter by herself, as an unwed single mother, would not have been thought realistic at the time.

The Private Lives of Elizabeth and Essex was about Elizabeth I, Queen of England, and her romance with one of her advisors. The studio helped to "age" Bette by shaving back her hairline. This was a tough film for Bette to do because her co-star, Errol Flynn, pinched her and made dirty remarks and gestures. Flynn also seemed bored with his work. To get through it herself, Bette fantasized that she was working instead with Laurence Olivier, the great English actor.

In 1941, Bette showed how much she was willing to do to make her films as good as they could be. *The Great Lie* had Bette's character fighting with another woman over the same man. Most stars did everything they could to make their own roles the most important one in each movie they made. In this film Bette thought that improving the part of the other woman, played by Mary Astor, would make a better movie.

Mary and Bette got together and worked out how the two women they played should act. They wanted them to be believable. They did this while the picture was being made, rewriting the script as they went along. The result was an Oscar for Best Actress for Mary Astor.

In 1942 Bette made a romantic drama called *Now, Voyager.* Her character, Charlotte Vale, is an ugly duckling. Her mother shelters her from life, but she meets a doctor who helps her to break away. Early in the film she is made up to look very plain and unattractive. Later, after she has a make-over, she is pretty. She meets a man named Jerry on a cruise and falls in love with him. But he's already married, although unhappily. In several romantic scenes, now famous, he lights two cigarettes in his mouth, one for each of them.

By the end of the movie, Charlotte has made friends with Jerry's daughter. She has some of the same emotional problems that Charlotte used to have. Charlotte becomes a kind of second mother to her. She and Jerry realize that, in a way, the girl

A poster from the film *Now, Voyager* (1942). Bette co-starred in this film with Paul Henreid.

During World War II, Bette was an active supporter of the Hollywood Canteen, a social club for people serving in the armed forces.

is "their" child. Jerry still wishes that he and Charlotte could live together and find happiness, but Charlotte knows that's not to be. As the movie ends, she looks up at the night sky and says, "Jerry, let's not ask for the moon when we have the stars."

Old Acquaintance, a 1943 film, had Bette playing Kit, a writer, and Miriam Hopkins playing Millie, a housewife and old friend of Kit. Millie wants something more out of life than just cleaning the house, cooking for her husband, and raising her child. She, too, becomes a writer. When she does, though, her marriage starts to fail. Her husband develops a crush on Kit, and tells her, "Our marriage has been headed for the rocks since Millie started to write." Kit won't hurt her old friend, and she rejects Millie's husband, even though he does leave his wife.

Despite her success as a writer, Kit also has problems. She falls in love with a man ten years younger than herself. At first she turns down his proposal of marriage. Then, when she finally decides to marry him, he tells her that he has fallen in love with a younger woman. One of the messages this movie sends is that women can't have a career *and* a family. It also shows what happens to a woman who dares to love a younger man—she can only be hurt. This is what many people then believed.

While some of Bette's films in these years dealt with problems of everyday life, others focused on troubles in the outside world. World War II started in 1939, and by 1941 America was at war with Germany, Italy, and Japan. In one of her films, *A Watch on the Rhine,* Bette played the wife of a man who fought the Nazis, the people who had come to power in Germany.

Bette also helped to set up a place in Hollywood where off-duty soldiers could relax. It was called the Hollywood Canteen. Soldiers could come there and dance with movie stars. The stars, who worked for free, also served them snacks. In 1943, Warner Brothers made a movie about the place, called *Hollywood Canteen,* in which Bette appeared.

The group running the Hollywood Canteen elected Bette president. Some people wanted to keep black soldiers at the canteen separate from whites. This custom, segregation, was then in force in the army. Bette wouldn't allow it at the Hollywood Canteen. "The blacks got the same bullets that the whites did," she reminded everyone. They should also be equal when the shooting stopped.

In *Mr. Skeffington* (1944), Bette switches roles and plays a frilly, fascinating character.

The End of an Era

In the mid-1940s, Bette Davis made three more soap opera-type films that critics and the public liked: *Mr. Skeffington, The Corn Is Green,* and *Deception.* But her time at the top was ending. The problem was her age. She was almost forty. Hollywood had few good parts for women who were not young. On the screen and in real life, women past this age, their courting and child-bearing days over, did not have major roles to play.

Bette was making fewer films now, although her salary had reached its peak. In 1947, Bette Davis was the highest paid woman in America. That year she made $328,000, but she was becoming less valuable to Warner Brothers. Her recent films had not made much money. Now the studio was not so willing to give in when she argued with them. By 1949, Bette and the studio were close to parting.

While making *Beyond the Forest* that year, Bette fought with the director of the movie. She tried to go over him to Jack Warner, head of the studio. When Bette complained to Warner about the director, she said, "It's him or me." Warner replied "Okay Bette, it's you." The studio would not offer her another contract.

Beyond the Forest, Bette's fifty-second and last movie at Warner Brothers, summed up the type of roles that Bette had made famous. One critic said that the woman who Bette played was the kind who "nags, steals, cheats, and is altogether a no-good tramp." Looking at her in the light of today's values, however, she appears a little different, a bit more sympathetic.

Claude Rains played the male lead in *Mr. Skeffington* (1944).

Bette's character in the film lives in a small town. She's trapped in a bad marriage. The walls seem like they're closing in. In one scene, she looks around her house and says, "What a dump!" There seems to be no way out. She watches her husband try to catch a fish and she thinks to herself: "Go, go, little fishie, get out while you've still got the pep."

The woman takes a lover and tries to leave town with him. When an old man stands in their way, she kills him. She's found innocent at her trial. Then she becomes pregnant. She calls her pregnancy, which she doesn't want, "the mark of death." An abortion seems to be the only answer. She does it herself, and ends up killing herself. Bette's last line in the film is: "I can't stand it anymore."

Bette cried when she drove away from Warner Brothers for the last time. She said

Bette with her daughter B.D.

their parting was a "professional divorce." It was the end of a relationship that no longer worked.

Her private life wasn't going well either. Her second marriage to Arthur Farnsworth, a New England innkeeper, was crumbling. He was an alcoholic, there was little passion between them, and he was also unfaithful. One day, in 1943, he died suddenly, while walking on the street. An earlier blow to his head apparently played a role in his death.

Bette's next marriage was a disaster from the start. William Grant Sherry, an artist, threw a suitcase at her on their wedding night. He was "hot-tempered, brutal," according to Bette. She claimed that he once threw her down a flight of stairs and that things got so bad that she thought of killing herself.

Looking back at this relationship years later, Bette did recall one satisfying part of it. "I got a beautiful daughter from one of those awful marriages," she told an interviewer. Her daughter, Barbara Davis Sherry, was born in 1947. Bette soon dropped the child's last name and called her "B.D." (Bette's own initials). She goes by that name to this day.

Chapter 5

Life After Warner Brothers

Bette was now starting a new part of her life. She had become a mother, she no longer worked for Warner Brothers, and she was entering middle age. Bette said that turning forty was like "being hit by a truck." People thought of her as older. They did not think of actresses that age as glamorous, and there were fewer good parts for them.

Bette was lucky. She was offered a good part in a film. The movie was about the problems of an aging actress. The film, *All About Eve,* featured a character named Margo Channing who was something like Bette—sharp-tongued, independent, and turning forty.

"That picture saved my life," Bette would later say of *All About Eve.* The sharp comedy, with many funny lines that people still like to quote, would become a classic and win six Oscars, including the one for best picture. Bette herself did not win an award, although the reviewer for *Time* wrote that "it may be the best performance of her career." For the moment, at least, she was back in the spotlight.

A young actress in *All About Eve* pushes aside an older one and takes her place in a play. The older actress, Margo Channing, played by Bette, does not submit to this young upstart gracefully. "Peace and quiet is for libraries," she says. In one scene, at a party, she lets everyone know that she will not be pushed around. She announces: "Fasten your seatbelts—it's going to be a bumpy night!" Through Margo, Bette was again able to portray a woman who did things a little differently. (One way Margo

In *All About Eve* (1950), Bette is an aging actress who feels threatened by an up-and-coming younger actress.

was different from most other women of her time is that she had a romance with a younger man.)

Family Life Revisited

In real life, Bette and the actor who played the younger man, Gary Merrill, were seeing one another. Bette's marriage to William Grant Sherry was slipping away. He complained of being a "housewife." "I have dinner ready when she gets home," he grumbled. "I take off her shoes and bring her slippers and a drink." With the bitter feelings came more violence and, finally, a divorce.

Bette and her husband Gary Merrill, with their two children.

Bette married Gary Merrill in 1951, and eventually they adopted two children, Michael and Margot. Margot, they soon discovered, was mentally retarded and had to be placed in a special school.

Bette was not able to follow *All About Eve* with similar successes. *The Star,* which she made in 1952, was about a washed-up actress trying to make a comeback. The plot was uncomfortably close to the life Bette now led in her mid-forties.

Next Bette appeared on the stage in a musical called *Two's Company.* While performing in Detroit she fainted. "Well, you

Bette again plays Elizabeth I in *The Virgin Queen* (1955).

can't say I didn't fall for you," she joked to the audience when she got up. But the fainting spell was no joke. It came from a disease she had developed in her jaw. As it got worse, she had to temporarily retire from acting.

Bette and Gary bought a house in Maine. They called it "Witch Way" because

of the nastiness of some of Bette's characters, and also because they weren't sure
which direction their lives and careers
would now take. Bette seemed happy
being a mother and living a life then more
typical of women. Beneath the surface,
however, there was already trouble. As
Bette put it, Gary "was not always sober."
Before long, he and Bette were having
violent fights.

In 1955 Bette returned to films, again
playing Queen Elizabeth I of England. In
The Virgin Queen, her head was shaved to
make her look older. A year later she
played a plain Bronx housewife in *A Catered
Affair.*

She also began to make television appearances. Many movie stars felt that TV
drama was put together too quickly and
could not be as artistic as films made the
old-fashioned way in Hollywood. Bette
thought that was silly. She remembered
just how fast movies used to be made in
Hollywood in the 1930s and 1940s. Working as hard as she did back then, she often
got good reviews for her TV performances.
As a result, Bette eventually won several
Emmy Awards for acting in TV dramas.

In 1957, a fall put Bette in the hospital
with a broken back. The period of the

late1950s was also made difficult by the decline of her marriage to Gary Merrill. When it ended in 1960, she saw herself a "complete failure as a wife." She felt that it was her last chance to live a traditional family life.

Aging in a World that Loves Only Youth

As she aged, Bette was offered even fewer good screen parts, although she did do well in a play called *The Night of the Iguana,* by noted playwright Tennessee Williams. In 1962 a role in a horror movie brought her career back to life. The producers of *Whatever Happened to Baby Jane?* had the idea of using her and Joan Crawford, an actress famous for her romantic roles in the 1940s. Both aging stars decided to take a chance. They would settle for low salaries, but they would also get part of the profits. The movie, about two old sisters and a murder that one of them has committed, was a surprise hit.

Besides the film, people also talked about how Bette and Joan fought with each other. It soon developed into a legendary Hollywood feud. Bette claimed that Joan was so vain that she wanted to look glamorous in the film even though it was sup-

Bette and Joan Crawford play two old sisters in *Whatever Happened to Baby Jane?* (1962).

posed to be a horror movie. Bette was nominated for an Oscar and, she says, Joan tried to convince people not to vote for her (she didn't win). Bette, often speaking frankly in public as she got older, called herself and Joan "two old broads." Crawford asked her to stop it. She claimed that Bette wanted all the glory. She said that Bette called her "a movie star and referred to herself as an actress."

The feud helped to keep Bette's name in the papers. She also got her name in print through a more direct way. Despite the success of *Baby Jane,* Bette was still getting few good offers for films. To call attention to herself, Bette, one of Hollywood's greatest stars, put a classified ad in a show business newspaper. The ad ran under "Situation Wanted, Women Artists." She mentioned her "thirty years experience" and added, "Wants steady employment in Hollywood." Many people were shocked that a great star would do such a thing. Some thought it was a joke. Others said it was a publicity stunt to call attention to *Whatever Happened to Baby Jane?*

Bette still needed a good deal of money to support her mother and retarded daughter, who remained in a special home, and to pay for her emotionally ill sister's hospital bills. The actress took just about any work she could get, and this led to her appearance in a string of bad films. These roles were not inspiring. Perhaps because of this, Bette's acting was not as good as it had been. One critic, Gene Ringgold, in a book about all of Bette's movies, wrote that in her work after the mid-1960s she "insisted on over-acting and hogging every scene in which she appeared."

By this time Bette was living off her past fame. She was a legend—the great female actress of the 1940s. She made frequent guest appearances on the Johnny Carson Show and other programs where she could talk about the past. In 1981 someone even recorded a hit song called "Bette Davis Eyes," which reminded people of her most famous feature.

Bette's earlier films kept running on television, gaining her young fans who did not know her at her peak. She began to make theater appearances to meet her fans. Instead of acting she sang a few songs, read poetry, told stories about the old days in Hollywood, and answered questions from the audience. She was billed as "*Miss* Bette Davis," a sign of respect given to only a few of the greatest stars.

At a typical appearance, she joked with the audience. One person asked her why she didn't get a face-lift, an operation to smooth over the many wrinkles on her skin. "Who would I be kidding?" she replied. If a film were made about her life, who should play Bette Davis? "Someone peculiar," she said.

In many of her movies Bette now no longer had the lead role. One exception, *Skyward,* a TV film she starred in, in 1980,

In one of Bette's last films, ***The Whales of August*** **(1987), she and Lillian Gish play two sisters.**

got good reviews. In the film she played a pilot who taught a disabled girl how to fly a plane. She also had a memorable role in her last, major full-length film, *The Whales of August.* The film portrays two elderly sisters who struggle with their loves and jealousies of each other.

Bette's natural frankness insured that she would not have a completely quiet old age. "I have never learned when to shut my mouth," she said of her reputation for always saying whatever was on her mind. Directors and other movie people who worked with her knew all about that. What Bette could not have guessed was that her daughter was also going to speak about what was on *her* mind.

In 1985 B.D. published a book called *My Mother's Keeper.* In it she described her mother as selfish, mean, often drunk, depressed, and sometimes suicidal. She wrote that Bette had provoked her husbands into mistreating her. B.D. also accused Bette of trying to break up her marriage. There's no way of telling how much of this portrait of a monster was true.

In her own book, *This 'N That,* Bette replied. She wrote that B.D. always liked to exaggerate and had a talent for "fiction." She also claimed that her daughter was mixing up the Bette Davis in the movies with the mother B.D. had in real life. A few years earlier Bette had admitted that she had "a special ability to play a bitch." Did that mean she *was* one? "No one who's really a bitch dares to expose herself," Bette said. The split between mother and daughter was to be final.

Bette had a bout with cancer in the early 1980s. She recovered, but the disease reappeared later in the decade. She died in 1989 at the age of 81.

"I suppose I'm larger than life," Bette Davis once said. Having appeared on the big screen in movie theaters for several decades and been nominated for more Oscars—ten—than any other actress helped to make her seem like a giant.

Bette blazed a trail for other actresses to follow. In the thirties, it was not unusual for men to play unlikable characters, such as gangsters, and make them seem real and interesting. Bette was one of the first to do this for female roles. She also led the way for actresses to insist on having a say in which roles studios would let them play.

Bette said that her idea of acting was to magnify everything. "Did I ever try to be low-key?" she asked. "Never, never, never!" But her success in her best years, the mid-

Two movie legends, Bette Davis and Jimmy Stewart.

1930s through the early 1950s, was at least partly based on the way she portrayed something that came from everyday life. It was the thoughts, feelings, hopes, and dreams of real women—her audience.

Bette once told her daughter: "There's only one way for a female to be recognized in this man's world . . . and that's to fight every inch of the way." To her secretary, she advised that "you must march to the beat of your own drum." Fighting to make it in a man's world and daring to be different were often traits of the characters Bette played. The women who saw her movies responded strongly to them, even if they weren't always able to act in their own lives the way Bette did in her films. Bette's performances touched them deeply.

Claude Rains as Mr. Skeffington in the 1944 movie of the same name told Bette's character "A woman is beautiful only when she is loved." Many women in darkened movie theaters must have nodded "yes" when Bette replied: "A woman is beautiful if she has eight hours of sleep and goes to the beauty parlor every day. And bone structure has a lot to do with it." The truth may have made men uncomfortable, but Bette Davis was usually willing to tell it.

Glossary

Explaining New Words

casting Deciding who will play which parts in a movie.

critic One who reviews movies, giving an opinion about them and the actors and actresses who appear in them.

director The person who supervises the shooting of each scene of a movie.

long-term contract An agreement in which an actor or actress agrees to work only for one studio for several years.

movie studio A company set up to make at least several films every year; it is also the buildings where the films are made.

Oscar The awards given every year for the best work by people who make movies—including best picture, actor and actress, and director.

preview An advance showing of a movie to see how audiences react to it.

producer The person who manages the business side of making a movie.

publicity Getting a movie mentioned in newspapers and magazines and talked about on radio and TV so that people will hear about it and want to see it.

screen test A sample scene filmed to see how an actor does in a role.

star billing The placing of an actor's name above the title of a movie.

studio system The system—in effect until the mid-1950s—in which a few Hollywood companies controlled almost everything about making movies, including which movies would be made and who would star in them.

take The filming of a scene; many takes of the same scene are often required before it's good enough to become part of the movie.

For Further Reading

Davis, Bette (with Michael Herskowitz).
	This 'N That. New York: G.P.
	Putnam's Sons, 1987.
Haskell, Molly. *From Reverence to Rape: The
	Treatment of Women in the Movies,* 2nd
	ed. Chicago: University of Chicago
	Press, 1987.
Higham, Charles. *Bette: The Life of Bette
	Davis.* New York: Macmillan, 1981.
Hyman, B.D. *My Mother's Keeper.* New York:
	Berkley, 1986.

Kay, Karyn, and Gerald Peary. *Women and the Cinema: A Critical Anthology.* New York: Dutton, 1977.

Ringgold, Gene. *Bette Davis: Her Films and Career.* Secaucus, New Jersey: The Citadel Press, 1966 (revised and updated, 1985).

Rosen, Marjorie. *Popcorn Venus: Women, Movies & the American Dream.* New York: Coward, McCann & Geoghegan, 1973.

Stine, Whitney. *Mother Goddam: The Story of the Career of Bette Davis,* with a running commentary by Bette Davis. New York: Hawthorn Books, 1974.

Vermilye, Jerry. *Bette Davis.* New York: Galahad Books, 1973.

Wayne, Jayne Ellen. *Crawford's Men.* New York: Prentice-Hall, 1988.

Index

Photo credits:
Cover, pages 4, 34: Kobal Collection; pps. 5, 12, 15, 19, 20, 44:
The Bettman Archive; pps. 8, 46, 48, 49: Bette Davis Collection,
Boston University Libraries; pps. 11, 14, 29, 42: courtesy of the
Hearst Collection, Department of Special Collections, USC
Libraries, Los Angeles; pps. 16, 28, 35, 40, 41, 47, 50, 53, 56:
Photofest; pps. 23, 36, 38, 58: UPI/Bettman Newsphotos.

Photo Research by Photosearch, Inc.